For John, my twin and dear friend, who first brought me to Cape Ann.
~ M. F.

To all the people who came before my time, who have carved out a home in this part of the world, the land of granite and saltwater.
~ S. D. K.

ISBN 978-1-7322085-5-1
First Edition, July 2023
Published by The Paper Mermaid, LLC
57 Main Street, Rockport, MA 01966

www.papermermaid.com

a day in
GLOUCESTER
Massachusetts

Scenes from America's Oldest Seaport

The Paper Mermaid Press
Rockport, MA

a day in GLOUCESTER

Pictures by
Mary Faino

Words by
S.D. Kelly

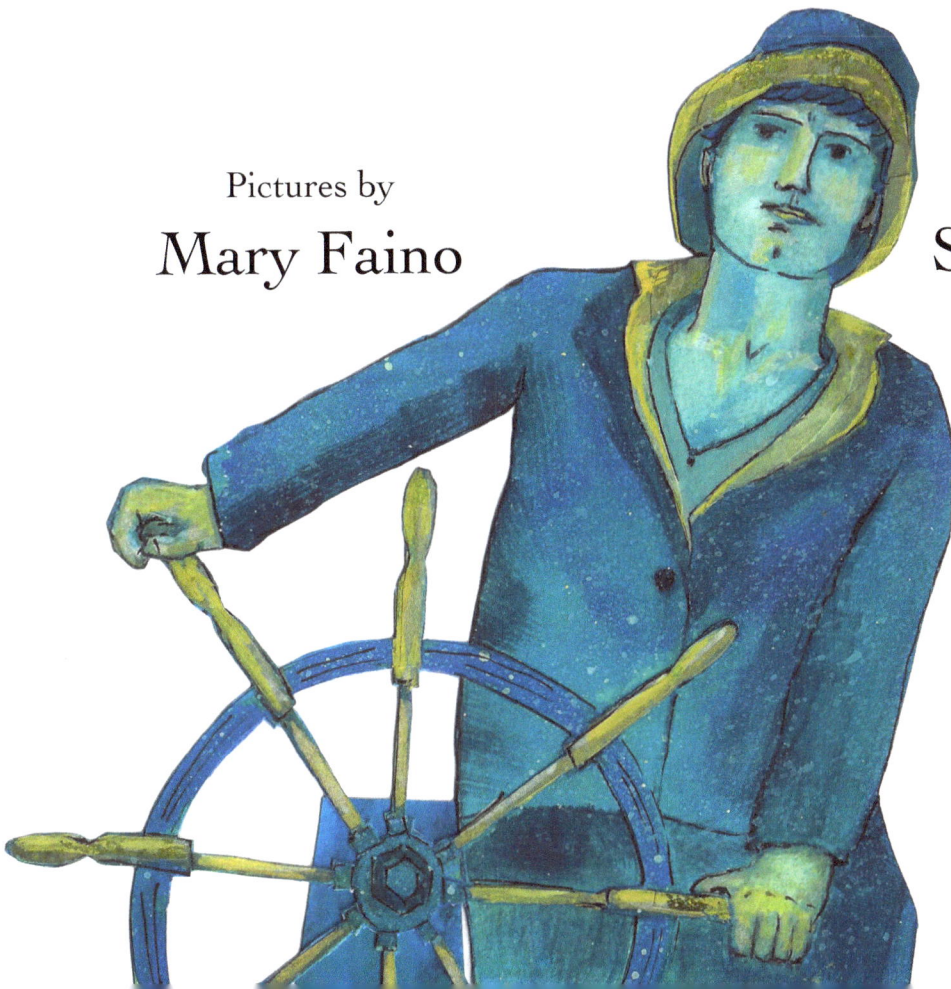

The moonlight is still on the water.

The cat, curled up, is still asleep.

Only the seagull is awake, perched on the wharf,

ready for the day, ready for the rising sun.

One boat heads out of the harbor. The seagull follows the boat.
Awake now, the cat watches. The water glows with morning light,
just as the sun comes up.

Now all the boats leave the harbor,
past the old factory, past the older island,
away from the city streets
and into the water.

It is time to find the fish,
time to pull and set the traps.
Time to set sail, just for fun.

Old men nod over their coffee.
The shops open up along the curve of Main Street.
The fresh light of the morning sun
makes the old port look new again.

Above the harbor, the sun hangs higher,
while down below, the beach fills with people.
They carry buckets and blankets.
They play in the water and the lapping waves.

Far out beyond the beach, beyond the trees,
beyond the rocks, beyond the breakwater,
whales are playing too.

And then there is the castle, sitting high
above the coast. The boats move across the water.
The waves hit the rocks below the arches.
They make a sort of music.

Come back down to the water's edge.
See the whales, the boats, the waves on rocks,
all painted on canvas.
Artwork for sale! Ice cream too!
Come, sit along the docks and dream.

ICE CREAM

The sun glows above the water.
See the sunset; take a walk along the Boulevard.
The Man at the Wheel is there, always alert,
working to return to port and to safe harbor.

Houses dot the hillside, high above the harbor.
Our Lady of Good Voyage is among them, standing between the bell towers.
She is as patient as the families at home, waiting and watching.
Boats go out and boats come in, under the sun and under the stars.

The bell tolls the hour. The city grows quiet.
Another day has ended. Back to port, back home,
the seagulls curl up to rest in the safety of their nest.
The time has come to say
goodnight.

The land that eventually became **Gloucester, Massachusetts**, has been used as a fishing ground by Indigenous people for thousands of years. It was home to the Pawtucket people in the period preceding European colonization. After the French explorer Samuel de Champlain came ashore in 1606, he created a map of the area, giving Gloucester its first European name, *le Beau Port:* the beautiful port. Several years later, in 1623, colonists established a permanent fishing outpost before formally incorporating as a town in 1642. They named the town after a city in England called Gloucester, though it is still considered to be *le beau port*.

Gloucester Harbor   pp. 7–11
Gloucester is the oldest seaport on the East Coast. Fishing boats (and pleasure boats too) have been coming and going in these waters for hundreds of years.

Paint Factory   p. 10
For close to 200 years, the old Paint Factory has been a landmark on the harbor. The factory was an important part of seafaring history with the production of a special paint for ships that changed the maritime industry.

Schooners   p.11
Another iconic sight in and around Gloucester Harbor are its schooners, with their distinctive rigging. The city was known as a shipbuilding center, with the first American Schooner built in 1713. Though no longer used for fishing, a few beautiful schooners still ply the waters of the harbor.

The West End of Main Street   pp. 12–13
Gloucester has seen many waves of immigrants from various countries over the generations. As Italians settled in Gloucester, the West End became known for featuring delicious Italian pastries, bread, and coffee.

Half Moon Beach   pp. 14–15
The curve of sand along one of the beaches at Stage Fort Park resembles a crescent moon. The beach is almost hidden below the rugged hillside, which adds to its beauty.

Whale Watching   pp. 16–17
Gloucester's close proximity to Stellwagen Bank National Marine Sanctuary makes the city one of the best places for whale watching in America.

Hammond Castle   pp. 18–19
Inventor John Hays Hammond, Jr. built his unique home and laboratory overlooking Gloucester in the 1920s. The beautiful medieval-style stone arches frame an iconic view of the New England coastline.

Rocky Neck   pp. 20–21
Rocky Neck has been a haven for artists and writers for many generations. Artists such as Winslow Homer and Edward Hopper have lived, worked, and visited Rocky Neck for inspiration – a tradition that continues to this day.

The Man at the Wheel Statue   pp. 22–23
"The Man at the Wheel" was sculpted by Leonard Caske in 1923 in celebration of Gloucester's 300th anniversary. It honors the courage of the many generations of Gloucester fishing families, making a very dangerous living at sea. The plaque on the monument references a poetic passage from the Bible, which reads:
> *They that go down to the sea in ships, that do business in great waters;*
> *These see the works of the Lord, and his wonders in the deep.*
> *Psalm 107: 23-24*

Our Lady of Good Voyage   pp. 24–25
Our Lady of Good Voyage is named for the Madonna, mother of Jesus. Portuguese fishermen, who had settled in Gloucester on a hill overlooking the harbor, built the church in her honor. The Madonna is depicted as cradling a boat in her arms, keeping the fishermen safe as they make their way back to port.

www.ingramcontent.com/pod-product-compliance
Lightning Source LLC
Chambersburg PA
CBHW042021090426

42811CB00016B/1701